ANTIQUE DINNER RECIPES

For all seasons

ANTIQUE DINNER RECIPES

For all seasons

AN 18TH CENTURY SELECTION

EMMA WOOD

CONSTANTIA BOOKS

©Constantia Books, 1987
All rights reserved
ISBN 0-930614-02-X
Library of Congress Catalogue Card No. 86-72035
Printed in the United States of America

Published by Constantia Books
40 Carwall Avenue
Mount Vernon, NY 10552

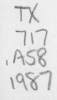

INTRODUCTION

Here's a bouquet of culinary delights from prosperous, romantic 18th century Britain. Celebrated traditional dishes and new creations from the hands of native cooks and imported French chefs. Temptations and promised pleasures for late twentieth century palates.

Dinner in that leisured world was very generous in quantity and high in quality. Appetites were larger than those of today and a typical meal comprised at least two elaborate courses of assorted meats, fish, fowl, vegetables and sweets. Artistic presentation of each dish was also a requisite.

Our collection of recipes comes from cookbooks published in England and Scotland between 1700 and 1800. Many Colonial American families were familiar with the recipes.

The recipes in this book will make an average of 4 servings.

A setting of six elegant dishes

CONTENTS

SPRING
First Course

ASPARAGUS SOUP

½ pound green peas

1 large celeriac, chopped

1 large onion, chopped

1 tablespoon minced parsley

1 sprig each fresh thyme and marjoram (or ⅛ teaspoon each, dried)

2 cups beef broth

1 pound asparagus, cut into ¼ inch pieces

Pepper and salt

Cayenne pepper

Several spinach leaves, finely chopped

PUT peas, celeriac, onion, parsley, herbs and broth into a pot. Bring to boil, cover, and simmer 1 hour. Strain into a bowl and set liquid aside. Mash solids through a sieve or puree in food processor. Return liquid and puree to pot and add asparagus, pepper, salt and cayenne. Cover and simmer 1 hour. Stir in spinach 15 minutes before serving.

VEAL IN CREAM

3 pounds boneless loin of veal	*1 tablespoon butter*
Salt	*1 tablespoon flour*
5 large garlic cloves	*1 tablespoon lemon juice*
1 quart milk	*1 teaspoon concentrated meat essence*

PLACE veal in a bowl and sprinkle with salt. Peel and bruise garlic, add to milk, and heat to boiling point. Pour over veal. Marinate 6 hours, turning several times. Drain, reserving milk, and place meat in a roasting pan. Roast 3 hours in 350-degree oven, using milk-garlic mix for basting. In a saucepan melt butter, add flour, lemon juice, meat essence and 1 cup basting liquid, stirring constantly. Bring to a boil, then lower heat and simmer 15 minutes. Slice the veal, arrange on a platter and top with sauce.

SAVOURY RICE

1¾ cups chicken broth   *Pepper and salt*
1 onion, chopped   ¾ cup long grain rice
¼ teaspoon mace

COMBINE ingredients, except rice, in a saucepan. Bring to boil and simmer 5 minutes. Boil again, stir in rice, cover, lower heat and cook 30 minutes.

A FRICASEY OF KIDNEY BEANS

1 cup kidney beans   ¼ cup minced parsley
1 pound onions, sliced   ¼ teaspoon thyme
1 cup beef broth
1 tablespoon butter   ½ teaspoon nutmeg
1 carrot, chopped   *Pepper and salt*

SOAK beans, covered in water, overnight. Drain. Place beans in pan, cover in fresh water and simmer over low heat 3 hours. Drain beans and set them aside. Brown onions in butter in a separate pan, then add carrot, parsley, thyme and broth and cook until contents are soft. Drain, set liquid aside, and mash through sieve or puree in food processor. Mix liquid, puree and beans together and stir in nutmeg and seasoning. Heat through before serving.

TO BROIL A SHAD

3 tablespoons butter

½ cup sorrel leaves

1 tablespoon parsley, minced

1 teaspoon chervil, minced

1 teaspoon chives, minced

1 cup heavy cream

¼ teaspoon nutmeg

Pepper and salt

1½ pounds shad fillets

MELT 2 tablespoons butter, add sorrel, parsley, chervil and chives, and cook until very soft. Heat cream to boil, add nutmeg and stir in sorrel. Season to taste and keep warm. Melt remaining butter and brush onto shad. Broil shad until it flakes easily with a fork, then remove it to a platter. Spoon sauce over fish.

A THATCHED-HOUSE PYE

2 ounces vermicelli

4 tablespoons butter

Puff pastry

4 squab (or 4 chicken thighs)

Pepper and salt

BREAK vermicelli into thirds and cook in boiling salted water 8 minutes. Drain. Butter a 1-quart baking dish and spread 2 tablespoons butter at bottom. Make even double-layer of vermicelli over butter. Line dish to brim with puff pastry. Rub seasoning over squab and put ½ tablespoon butter inside each. Fit birds, breast-side down, in dish and add pastry cover. Hand-pinch pastry where sides and top meet. Bake in 375-degree oven 1 hour. Turn out in serving dish. Vermicelli will form thatched-roof effect on top.

SPRING
Second Course

DUCK A-LA-MODE

1 5-pound duck, cut
in pieces

1 cup chicken broth

2 shallots, chopped

2 anchovy fillets,
chopped

1 bouquet garni (thyme,
parsley, bay leaf)

Butter, for browning

Seasoned flour

Lemon wedges

SKIN and de-fat duck and discard back. Combine in saucepan broth, wine, shallots, anchovies and bouquet garni. Heat, stirring until anchovies are dissolved. Melt butter in large casserole. Dredge duck pieces in flour and brown in butter. Pour sauce over duck, cover and simmer 1 hour. Remove duck to serving platter, discard bouquet garni and pour sauce over duck. Garnish with lemon wedges.

TO MAKE
SPINAGE TOASTS

2 pounds spinach

3 tablespoons butter

Salt

¼ cup currants

½ teaspoon nutmeg

4 slices toast,
buttered

WASH spinach but do not dry it. Melt 2 tablespoons butter in a pan and add spinach. Sprinkle with salt. Cover and cook on low heat 5 minutes. Turn spinach, moving top leaves to bottom, replace cover and raise heat level slightly. Cook until leaves are wilted, then drain and chop. Melt remaining butter in saucepan, add spinach, currants and nutmeg, stir and heat. Divide in equal portions and serve on pieces of toast.

TO FRY CRABS

1 pound crabmeat	3 egg yolks
2 tablespoons fresh breadcrumbs	Batter (see below)
2 tablespoons ground almonds	Clarified butter, for frying
¼ teaspoon nutmeg	Sauce (see below)
Pepper and salt	Crisp parsley

MIX together crabmeat, breadcrumbs, almonds, nutmeg, pepper, salt and egg yolks. Form 8 flat cakes and refrigerate ½ hour.

BATTER

½ cup flour	½ cup lukewarm water
Salt	3 egg whites
3 tablespoons melted butter	

COMBINE flour, salt, butter and water by stirring. Cover and let stand ½ hour. Beat egg whites until stiff and fold into mixture. Coat crabcakes with batter and fry until golden brown. Place on warm platter.

SAUCE

¼ pound crabmeat	1 tablespoon lemon juice
3 tablespoons melted butter	½ teaspoon nutmeg
Juice of 2 oranges	

PUT ingredients in saucepan and warm over low heat. Pour sauce over cakes and garnish with crisp parsley.

PORTUGUESE EGGS

Juice of 2 large lemons

⅓ cup and 2 tablespoons sugar

½ tablespoon salt

4 beaten eggs

HEAT lemon juice, one-third cup of sugar and salt in a saucepan until sugar dissolves. Add eggs and stir steadily until creamy-thick. Remove to shallow baking dish, sprinkle with remaining sugar and glaze under broiler. Cool and chill before serving.

STRAWBERRIES WHOLE

1 quart strawberries

½ cup red currant jelly

Light cream

TAKE strawberries at room temperature and place in a bowl. Wash and hull them. Slowly heat jelly to boil in a saucepan, stirring constantly. Combine berries and sauce and stir several times with a spoon while letting the mix stand 2 hours. Top with cream at table.

TO MAKE KING CAKES

¾ cup butter

¾ cup sugar

2 egg yolks

1 tablespoon cream

1¼ cups flour

1 teaspoon mace

½ cup currants

BEAT the butter and sugar together until mix is light and fluffy. Combine egg yolks and cream, then stir in flour and mace and currants. Spoon the batter in small dollops onto 2 buttered baking sheets. Bake in 375-degree oven 12 to 15 minutes. Makes about 30 cakes.

10

SUMMER

First Course

VEGETABLE SOUP

½ cup butter

3 peeled, sliced cucumbers

3 heads chopped romaine lettuce

1 cup green peas

¼ cup minced parsley

1 large sliced onion

2 sprigs chopped fresh mint

Pepper and salt

MELT butter in a pan, then add other ingredients. Cook on low heat 30 minutes. Strain, reserving liquid, and puree vegetables. Return liquid and puree to pan, add 3 cups water, cover and let simmer 30 minutes.

ROAST LAMB

1 leg of lamb

1 bunch parsley

⅔ cup orange juice

⅓ cup lemon juice

SCORE lamb fat in a diamond pattern and fill scores with parsley. Roast in 325-degree oven, allowing ½ hour per pound. Baste with fruit juice mix.

SAUCE

3 tablespoons butter

2 cucumbers, peeled and sliced into ¼ inch pieces

1 sliced onion

½ cup chicken broth

1 teaspoon cider vinegar

1 teaspoon chopped mint

Pepper and salt

1 tablespoon butter mashed with 1 tablespoon flour

12

BROWN 2 tablespoons butter, add cucumbers and cook 1 minute. Remove cucumbers to a plate. Add onion and remaining butter to pan and cook 1 minute. Return cucumbers to pan, add stock, vinegar, mint and seasoning. Cover and simmer 15 minutes. Now add the butter and flour mix, a bit at a time, and cook 5 minutes uncovered. Serve in a sauce boat.

A GREEN-BEAN PUDDING

1 cup green beans, sliced thin	*Pepper and salt*
6 tablespoons butter	*Parsley-butter sauce (see below)*
3 tablespoons heavy cream	*4 slices Canadian-style bacon, cut into strips and fried crisp*
1 egg, separated	

PLACE beans, butter and cream in saucepan, cover and cook until beans are tender. Cool, then add the egg yolk and transfer the whole mass to a food processor and puree it. Whip the egg-white lightly, mix it into puree and add seasoning. Divide into 4 buttered custard cups and place in pan of 1-inch deep hot water. Bake in 400-degree oven 35 minutes. Let cool 5 minutes before unmolding onto plates. Top with parsley-butter sauce and garnish with bacon.

SAUCE

4 tablespoons butter	*Pepper and salt*
1 tablespoon parsley, minced	*1 teaspoon lemon juice*

CREAM the butter, then mix in the parsley and seasoning while adding lemon juice a little at a time. Chill before serving over the pudding.

TO DRESS MACKAREL

4 mackerel, heads and tails removed	4 bulbs fennel
4 tablespoons olive oil	3 tablespoons clarified butter
¼ teaspoon fennel seeds, crushed	2 teaspoons white wine vinegar
Pepper and salt	Crisp parsley (see below)

MAKE 3 diagonal scores on sides of fish. Combine oil, fennel seeds and seasoning and spoon over fish. Marinate 1 hour. Cook fennel bulbs in boiling water until tender, then drain and separate the layered parts. Line an oiled baking dish with half the fennel, place fish on it and top with the remaining fennel. Spoon marinade over the fish and bake in 375-degree oven 30 minutes. Melt butter and stir in vinegar. Make bed of fennel on serving platter, place fish on top and spoon sauce over it. Garnish with crisp parsley.

TO CRISP PARSLEY

SELECT very fresh sprigs, soak in ice water and pat dry with paper towel. Dip parsley in melted, clarified butter and roll around until lightly coated. Line a flat baking dish with several layers of paper towels. Place parsley pieces, individually, on dish and bake 15 minutes in pre-heated 350-degree oven.

BEEF A LA MODE

This dish was a very fashionable 18th century speciality. Some shops produced it exclusively from "secret" recipes. It could be eaten hot or cold. Here is a jellied version to be served cold.

¼ pound bacon

3 pounds rump or top-round beef, rolled and tied

2 onions, quartered

2 carrots, cut into 1-inch pieces

2 stalks celery, cut into 1-inch pieces

3 sprigs parsley

1 bay leaf

Salt

6 black peppercorns

3 whole cloves

3 whole allspice berries

1 blade mace

2 pounds soup bones, cracked

2 cups red wine

3 teaspoons gelatine

Capers and nasturtium flowers (garnishes)

PREHEAT oven to 325 degrees. Fry bacon in a casserole until browned, then remove. Brown beef on all sides in bacon fat, then remove. Add onions, carrots and celery and brown them slightly. Return beef and bacon to casserole and add seasoning and spices. Tuck bones next to meat, pour in wine and enough water to cover. Bring to boil, remove scum, cover and braise in oven 5 hours. Remove from pot and place in deep bowl. Strain stock over meat, cool, and refrigerate

overnight. Next day remove fat layer from stock, place meat on a platter, cut away string and fat. Now shred the meat, using two forks, and place on a wide, flat dish. Heat stock jelly until it melts, pour through sieve lined with dampened cheesecloth, and return to pan. Heat to a boil, then stir in gelatine and cook until it dissolves. Pour a coating of stock over the meat. Put remaining stock in a bowl, cool and refrigerate. When serving, chop extra jelly into small pieces and distribute over meat. Sprinkle capers over meat and decorate top with nasturtium flowers. Serves 8.

ARTICHOKE SUCKERS
THE SPANISH WAY

1 9-ounce pack frozen artichoke hearts, cut in half

4 tablespoons olive oil

1 tablespoon white wine-vinegar

2 egg yolks, beaten slightly

Pepper and salt

COMBINE artichokes, oil, vinegar and 2 tablespoons water, and cook, covered, 15 minutes. Stir in egg yolks and season to taste.

16

SUMMER
Second Course

CHICKEN WITH PEASE AND LETTUCE

1 pound green peas

1 sprig each parsley, scallion and thyme, tied together

2 young chickens, trussed

3 small heads Boston lettuce

3 tablespoons butter

Pepper and salt

PLACE peas in a saucepan that will accommodate the chickens, and dot with 1 tablespoon butter. Lay tied herbs on peas, fit chickens in side by side, breast down, and dot with tablespoon of butter. Wash lettuces but do not dry them, cut in half and lay over chickens. Add remaining butter, sprinkle with pepper and salt, and pour in half-cup water. Cover and cook over low heat 1 hour. To serve, untruss chickens and place in shallow bowl, breast up, remove herbs, surround with peas and lettuce, and fill dish to capacity with broth.

LEMON SALADE

5 large thick-skinned lemons

1 cup sugar

1 cup dry sherry

1 cup white wine vinegar

PUT lemons in a pot of boiling water for 3 minutes, then drain. Peel lemons, including pith, in narrow 3-inch curls. Discard pulp. Soak peels in cold water 12 hours and drain. Boil them, covered in water, until tender. Drain and pack into quart jar. Combine sugar, sherry and vinegar and bring to a boil, then simmer and stir until sugar dissolves. Pour liquid over peels in jar, cover, and refrigerate 1 week.

FRY'D SELLERY

4 celery hearts	¼ teaspoon nutmeg
1 cup flour	Salt
3 egg yolks	Butter for frying
	2 tablespoons melted
1 cup white wine	butter

BOIL celery in salted water 10 minutes, drain, refresh in cold water and pat dry. Combine flour, egg yolks, wine, nutmeg and salt, stirring until smooth. Cover and let stand 30 minutes. Melt butter in a frying pan, dust celery with flour and dip into batter, then fry to golden brown. Top with melted butter at table.

BUTTERED SHRIMPS

1½ pounds raw shrimps, unshelled	½ teaspoon nutmeg
	Salt
2 cups white wine	2 eggs, beaten
2 tablespoons butter	4 slices toast

CLEAN shrimps and wash shells. Put shells and wine in a saucepan and boil until liquid is reduced by half. Strain, discard shells and put liquid in a clean pan. Add to the liquid shrimps, butter, nutmeg and salt and simmer over low heat until shrimps turn pink. Mix a tablespoon of hot liquid with the beaten eggs and add it to the pan to make a sauce. Continue cooking for a few minutes, while stirring gently, but do not allow to boil. Apportion toast on 4 plates, spoon shrimps over the toast and top with sauce.

RASBERY TART
WITH CREAM

1 pound puff pastry	1 teaspoon powdered sugar whisked into an egg white
1 quart raspberries	
½ cup sugar	2 egg yolks
	¾ cup heavy cream

ROLL-OUT pastry to ⅛-inch thickness and line a pie plate with half the amount. Fill well with berries, in mound form, and sprinkle with sugar. Make pastry top and decorate with leaf shapes using pastry scraps. Brush on sugar-and-egg mixture. While tart is baking (20 minutes in a 375-degree oven) mix the egg yolks and cream in a pan and heat to boil. Remove tart from oven, make gash with knife through top center of crust — making opening through which egg-cream mix can be spooned over the berries. Close gap and return tart to oven for another ten minutes.

TO MAKE
APRICOCK JUMBALLS

1 pound ripe apricots, peeled and pitted and chopped fine	Confectioner's sugar

COOK apricots in a cup of water until very soft. Beat in enough sugar to make stiff paste, roll into thin strips. Twist into bowknot shapes, place on a buttered baking sheet and bake in 200-degree oven until dry.

AUTUMN
First Course

CARROT SOUP

4 quarts beef broth

Beef bones

2 large onions,
chopped

1 chopped turnip

6 large carrots, peeled
and sliced

Cayenne pepper

MIX together broth, bones, onions and turnip in a pot. Bring to a boil, skim off scum, lower heat and simmer, covered, 3 hours. Strain, discard solids and return liquid to pot. Add carrots and simmer, uncovered, until carrots are soft. Strain, reserve the liquid, mash carrots through sieve or puree in food processor. Combine carrots with stock, then refrigerate overnight. Next day remove fat from surface and simmer soup until quite thick. Add cayenne to taste.

A LOIN OF PORK WITH ONIONS

4 pounds loin of pork

4 medium onions, sliced

1 tablespoon flour

1 tablespoon red wine
vinegar

3 teaspoons Dijon-style
mustard

FILL bottom of a roasting pan with onions. Place pork above, on rack, in a 350-degree oven. Roasting time is 3 hours but after 2¾ hours take meat from oven and transfer onions to saucepan. Return roast to oven. Stir onions and set on low heat. When pork is cooked, whisk together flour, vinegar and mustard and stir into onions. Heat onions several minutes longer and serve in separate dish to accompany pork.

RED CABBAGE

1 red cabbage, shredded	*1 slice ham*
1 cup and 2 tablespoons beef broth	*1 tablespoon butter*
	1 tablespoon sugar
½ cup red wine vinegar	*Pepper and salt*

PLACE cabbage, 1 cup broth, vinegar, ham and butter in a pot. Cover and simmer 3 hours. Uncover, stir in remaining broth, sugar and seasoning. Boil until liquid is largely reduced.

TO BROIL FRESH SALMON

6 tablespoons butter	*1 teaspoon minced capers*
2 tablespoons flour	
Salt	*¼ teaspoon nutmeg*
4 salmon steaks	*2 tablespoons white wine vinegar*
4 sliced leeks (white parts only)	
1 anchovy fillet, washed, dried and chopped	*Lemon wedges*

MELT 2 tablespoons butter, stir in 1 teaspoon flour and salt. Brush this over both sides of salmon, then set aside. Preheat broiler. Melt remaining butter in a pan, add leeks, anchovy and capers and cook gently until leeks soften and anchovy melts. Stir in remaining flour, nutmeg, vinegar and ½ cup of water. Cook 5 minutes, then lower heat. Broil salmon until light brown on each side. Pour sauce into serving dish, place salmon on it and garnish with lemon wedges.

TO BAKE MUSHROOMS

16 mushrooms

2 slices bacon,
chopped

3 tablespoons butter

3 tablespoons minced
parsley

2 tablespoons chopped
chives

Nutmeg

Pepper and salt

ARRANGE mushrooms, minus stems, flatside-down, in a baking dish. Fry bacon, then add butter and let it melt. Pour mix over mushrooms. Now add parsley, chives, nutmeg and seasoning and bake, uncovered, in 350-degree oven for 30 minutes.

A SALLET OF ANCHOVIES

4 2-ounce cans flat
fillets of anchovies

White wine

4 medium beets, cooked
and sliced

8 scallions

8 large sprigs parsley

¾ cup olive oil

Juice of 2 lemons

4 lemon slices

DRAIN anchovies, separate the fillets and lay them parallel in a shallow dish. Cover with wine and marinate 1 hour. Drain, distribute among 4 plates, accompanied by beets, scallions and parsley. Beat together oil and lemon juice and spoon over anchovies and beets. Garnish with lemon slices.

AUTUMN
Second Course

TO DRESS GAME BIRDS

4 rock cornish game hens

2 cups chicken broth

1 9-ounce package frozen artichoke hearts

1 tablespoon butter

1 10-ounce can whole chestnuts

1 cup red wine

½ teaspoon mace

Pepper and salt

Forcemeat (see below)

1 tablespoon butter mashed with 1 tablespoon flour

1 teaspoon lemon juice

TRUSS game hens and place, breast-side down, in large saucepan. Heat broth to boil and pour into pan, adding enough boiling water to half cover birds. Cover pan and simmer 30 minutes, then turn birds breast-side up, re-cover, and simmer 45 minutes. Cook artichoke hearts as directed on package, drain, add butter, and keep warm. Heat chestnuts separately. When birds are tender, remove to a platter, untruss, and keep warm. Bring liquid in pan to a simmer and poach forcemeat 5 minutes, then remove to platter containing birds. Add wine, mace and seasoning to liquid in pan and reduce the quantity to two cupfuls by cooking at high heat. Lower heat, stir in butter-flour mixture, little by little, until sauce thickens. Add lemon juice, then pour sauce over birds. Drain chestnuts and arrange, along with artichokes, around outer edge of serving platter.

FORC'D MEAT

½ pound ground veal

4 tablespoons fresh
   breadcrumbs

2 tablespoons shredded
   suet

1 slice ham, chopped

1 small onion, chopped

1 tablespoon parsley,
   minced

¼ teaspoon grated
   lemon peel

¼ teaspoon nutmeg

Salt

Cayenne pepper

1 egg, lightly
   beaten

PUT all ingredients into food processor and blend until smooth. Divide into 16 portions, then roll half into ball-shapes and half into sausage shapes.

TO STEW MUSSELS

4 pounds mussels

½ teaspoon nutmeg

2 cups fresh
   breadcrumbs

4 tablespoons melted
   butter

SCRUB and scrape mussels under cold running water, removing barnacles and beards. Discard any with cracked shell or which will not close. Place in a large pan with cover. Shake gently over high heat about 5 minutes to cause mussels to open. Discard those which do not open. Place remainder in a sieve set over a bowl. Add liquid from pan to bowl. Remove mussels from their shells and arrange in single layer in a shallow baking dish. Line sieve with double-thick, wet cheesecloth and strain liquid over mussels, and add a sprinkle of nutmeg. Toss breadcrumbs in butter, then spread over mussels. Brown under a hot broiler.

CABBAGE PUDDING

1 large cabbage	¼ teaspoon each mace, nutmeg and ginger, mixed
1 pound ground veal	
½ cup chopped white grapes	
	Pepper and salt
4 beaten egg yolks	4 tablespoons butter

PUT a head of cabbage in a pan with water to cover. Add salt and boil for 10 minutes (or until leaves are quite pliable). Drain and peel off 24 outer leaves, and put aside. Chop remaining cabbage and combine with veal, grapes, eggs and spices. Lay cabbage leaves flat and place some filling on each leaf. Roll and fold the leaves individually and pack them in a single layer in a shallow pan. Cover with boiling water, plus half the butter. Cover the pan with foil and simmer cabbage 30 minutes. Remove to a platter and keep warm. Boil remaining liquid on high heat to reduce sauce, then add remaining butter. Pour sauce over cabbage.

PISTACHIO NUT CREAM

1 cup chopped, blanched pistachio nuts (save some for garnish)	2 egg yolks
	½ cup sugar
¼ cup chopped, candied orange peel	2 cups light cream
	Green food coloring

MINCE nuts and orange peel into a fine paste in a food processor. Mix the egg, sugar, cream, nut mix and coloring (light green) in a saucepan. Cook, stirring steadily, over low heat, until custard thickens. Spoon into glasses and chill. Garnish with nuts.

A FINE SAFFRON CAKE

½ teaspoon saffron
threads

¾ cup milk

2 packets active dry
yeast

3 cups unbleached flour

½ cup sugar

½ teaspoon each
powdered cloves, mace
cinnamon

½ cup butter, melted

1 egg, beaten

1 tablespoon rosewater

1 tablespoon caraway
seeds

PUT saffron on an ovenproof plate and heat in a hot oven 5 minutes. Heat milk to a boil. Crumble saffron and put into small bowl, pour a little milk over it and let stand 15 minutes. Combine remaining milk, at room temperature, with the yeast, stir it and let stand 15 minutes. Then whisk it to a creamy froth. Mix flour, sugar and spices in a bowl, stir in yeast mix, butter, egg, saffron, rosewater and caraway seeds — and knead briskly for 10 minutes. Place in buttered bowl and turn it to make sure top is buttered. Cover and set in a warm place, to allow dough to double in size (about 2½ hours). Punch the dough to reduce its volume, then divide in half and place each piece in a warm, buttered charlotte mold. Cover, put in a warm place and permit the dough to rise again until it nearly reaches the top of the mold. Bake in a 375-degree oven 30 minutes.

SOUFFLE OF RICE
AND APPLES

¼ cup long grain rice

1 pint half-and-half
cream

½ teaspoon cinnamon

¼ teaspoon grated
lemon peel

1 egg beaten

Puff pastry

Apple marmalade
(see below)

4 egg whites

Confectioner's sugar

BRING a saucepan of water to boil, add rice and boil 1 minute. Drain, add cream, cinnamon and lemon peel, bring to boil, then lower heat and simmer, stirring, until cream is absorbed. Cool, transfer to a buttered 1-quart souffle dish, and brush the rice and top of dish with egg. Also rim top with pastry collar 1−1½ inches high, and brush with egg. Now spoon-in the apple marmalade, beat the egg whites until they will form soft peaks to top off the souffle. Sift confectioner's sugar overall and bake in a 375-degree oven for 30 minutes. Serve warm.

APPLE MARMELADE

1 pound cooking apples

1 cup sugar

¼ teaspoon grated lemon
peel

CUT apples into quarters or eighths and place in saucepan with 2 tablespoons water. Cook over low heat until soft, then mash through a sieve. Melt sugar in ¼ cup water, add apple pulp and lemon peel, and simmer, while stirring, for 15 minutes. Cool slightly before spooning onto souffle. (Makes about 1 cup.)

WINTER
First Course

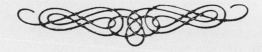

A NICE WHET
BEFORE DINNER

1 can anchovy fillets

4 slices fried, crustless
   bread, cut into thirds

¼ pound grated Cheshire
   cheese

2 tablespoons minced
   parsley

2 tablespoons melted
   butter

PLACE a washed and dried anchovy fillet on each
piece of bread, arranged on an ovenproof platter. Mix
cheese and parsley, sprinkle over fillets and pour
butter on top. Broil until cheese melts and top is light
brown.

TO MAKE PEASE SOOP

1 cup split peas

1 onion, chopped

4 anchovy fillets

1 tablespoon butter,
   mashed with 1 table-
   spoon flour

1 cup celery, sliced

3 leaves spinach
   chopped

1 teaspoon dried mint

Croutons

PRE-SOAK peas, if directions specify, then combine
peas, onion, anchovies and pepper in 3 pints water.
Cover and simmer 2 hours and drain, reserving liquid.
Mash solids through sieve or puree in food processor
and return liquid and puree to pot. Heat, stir in
butter-flour mixture, gradually, until soup thickens.
Add celery, spinach and mint and simmer 15 minutes.
Garnish with croutons.

TO DRESS A FILLET
OF BEEF

2½ pounds filet of beef

2 tablespoons melted
butter

1½ cups fresh bread-
crumbs

¼ cup minced parsley

1 teaspoon grated
lemon peel

½ teaspoon thyme

½ teaspoon nutmeg

Pepper and salt

½ pound sliced bacon

1 cup red wine

TAKE beef at room temperature and remove fat.
Preheat oven to 450 degrees. Brush beef with butter,
then coat it with a blend of crumbs, parsley, lemon
peel, thyme, nutmeg and seasoning. Wrap the beef in
bacon strips fastened with toothpicks. Put meat in a
roasting pan on oven rack. Mix wine with a cup of
water, heat it, then pour into meat pan. Roast 1 hour,
basting often. Remove to a platter and slice. Skim off
fat and spoon gravy over beef. Serves 6.

A POMATE OF PARSNIPS

2 pounds parsnips

¾ cup heavy cream

6 tablespoons soft butter

2 tablespoons brown
sugar

1 tablespoon lemon
juice

2 slices bread, fried in
butter, cut in triangles

PEEL parsnips and cut into 1-inch pieces. Cook in
boiling salted water 20 minutes. Puree in food processor. Combine puree and other ingredients, except
bread, in a double-boiler. Simmer and stir until well
blended. Arrange bread along edges of serving dish.

33

CABBAGE FORCE-MEAGRE

(with meatless stuffing)

1 2½ pound cabbage	2 tablespoons fresh breadcrumbs
2 hard-boiled eggs, whites and yolks separated (hold 1 yolk for sauce)	1 tablespoon white wine vinegar
½ pound flounder filets	1 raw egg
¼ cup minced parsley	Pepper and salt
⅛ cup butter, softened	Sauce (see below)

BLANCH cabbage in boiling water 15 minutes. Drain. Trim off stalk and stand cabbage stalk-side down. Carve hole about 3 inches wide at top of cabbage and scoop out contents to about ⅔ of depth. Discard core section, chop remainder and set aside. Chop egg whites. Combine chopped cabbage, 1 egg yolk, flounder, parsley, breadcrumbs, butter, vinegar, raw egg and seasoning in a food processor and mix until smooth. Stir in chopped egg whites, then stuff cabbage with the mix. Wrap cabbage in doubled cheesecloth, tie at top and place in pot. Pour sauce around bottom of wrapped cabbage. Cover pot and simmer 2 hours. Remove cabbage, cut away cheesecloth, then place in shallow serving dish. To serve, cut cabbage in pie-shape wedges and pour sauce around bottom of each serving. Serves 6.

SAUCE

⅛ cup butter, softened

1 onion, chopped

1 tablespoon white wine vinegar

1 cup sliced mushrooms

1 tablespoon flour

⅛ teaspoon each powdered cloves and mace

1 hard-boiled egg yolk

Pepper

MELT the butter in a saucepan, add onion, and cook until onion is soft. Add mushrooms and cook 1 minute. Stir in flour, vinegar, spices and pepper. Mash egg yolk and mix with 1 cup water, then combine with onion and mushrooms. Bring to boil, then pour sauce around base of cabbage.

TO MAKE A RAGOO OF ONIONS

2 cups pearl onions

2 large onions, chopped fine

½ cup butter

1 tablespoon flour

½ cup beef broth

Pepper and salt

1 teaspoon Dijon-style mustard

½ cup fresh breadcrumbs, browned in butter

FRY onions in butter until lightly browned, then stir in flour, broth and seasoning. Cover and simmer until pearl onions are tender and chopped onions have dissolved. Stir in mustard. Top with breadcrumbs.

WINTER
Second Course

PETIT PATTIES

½ pound turkey breast

1 slice Canadian-style bacon

2 tablespoons butter

2 tablespoons fresh breadcrumbs

1 egg yolk

¼ teaspoon thyme

¼ teaspoon nutmeg

Salt

White pepper

4 tablespoons heavy cream

2 tablespoons minced parsley

1 pound puff pastry

1 teaspoon confectioner's sugar dissolved in 1 egg white

CUT turkey, bacon and butter into small pieces and puree in food processor, in combination with breadcrumbs, egg yolk, thyme, nutmeg and seasoning. Move to a bowl and stir in cream and parsley. Roll out pastry ⅛-inch thick and cut into 32 squares. Distribute half the squares on two ungreased baking sheets and place a spoonful of filling on each. Wet edges of squares with cold water, then cover each with a plain square. Crimp the edges, trim, and brush each with egg-sugar glaze. Bake in pre-heated 375-degree oven 30 minutes. Serve hot or cold.

A RAGOO OF OYSTERS

2 *dozen oysters with*
  their liquid

2 *tablespoons butter*

1 *shallot, minced*

4 *egg yolks*

¼ *teaspoon nutmeg*

4 *slices toast, crusts*
  removed, cut into
  triangles

Lemon slices

DRAIN oysters and reserve liquid. Melt butter, add shallots and cook until soft. Add oyster liquid and reduce its volume by half by cooking on high heat. Lower heat, mix egg yolks with 2 tablespoons liquid from pan, and add this to pan to thicken sauce. Now add oysters and nutmeg and heat several minutes longer — but do not allow to boil. Pour into a serving dish and garnish with toast and lemon slices.

FRIED GOURDS

2 *pounds Hubbard,*
  butternut or acorn
  squash

1 *tablespoon butter*

1 *teaspoon lemon juice*

Salt

1 *egg, slightly*
  beaten

2 *cups fresh bread-*
  crumbs

Lard for frying

Pepper and salt

REMOVE skin, seeds and fiber from squash and cut into 1½-inch pieces. Place in saucepan with ½ cup water, butter, lemon juice and salt. Cover and simmer 20 minutes. Drain. Dip squash in egg and breadcrumbs, heat ½-inch of lard in frying pan and cook until golden brown. Season to taste.

TO MAKE GINGER-BREADS

1 cup flour	½ teaspoon salt
½ cup sugar	½ cup butter
2 teaspoons ginger	¼ cup molasses
1 teaspoon dried lemon peel	2 teaspoons candied orange peel, chopped

COMBINE flour, sugar, ginger, lemon peel and salt in a bowl. Combine butter and molasses separately and cream them thoroughly, then add to the bowl, followed by the chopped orange peel. Using a round-bladed knife, blend the mixture into a grainy dough. Wrap in foil and chill 2 hours. Form 1-inch size flat cakes and bake 15 minutes in a 350-degree oven.

COFFEE CREAM, MUCH ADMIRED

2 cups heavy cream	⅓ cup brown sugar
½ cup very strong coffee	1 envelope unflavored gelatine

HEAT the coffee combined with 1 cup cream, then stir in sugar and gelatine until they dissolve. Remove from heat, stir in remaining cream and pour into a serving bowl. Chill.

CHEESE AND ALMOND CAKES

8 ounces cottage cheese

2 eggs, beaten

¼ cup brandy

1 tablespoon melted butter

1 teaspoon almond extract

½ teaspoon grated lemon peel

Puff pastry

PRESS cheese through a sieve or puree in food processor. Beat in eggs, brandy, butter, almond extract and lemon peel. Line 12 muffin tins with pastry and spoon-in filling. Bake in 375-degree oven 30 minutes. Turn out to cool on a rack.

DRINKS

Assorted beverages were prominent and plentiful in the 18th century dining room. Wine glasses were kept filled all through dinner and beyond. The English favored port with dinner or supper and our Colonial ancestors preferred madeira. Other choices included ale, beer, cider, claret, punch and sherry. Also brandy and rum. Light drinks for the young or concoctions for top celebrations, such as the following, were also in vogue.

PUNCH FOR YOUNG LADIES

¾ cup sugar	½ cup lime juice
2 cups brandy	Juice of 1 orange
1 cup white wine	Juice of 1 lemon

BOIL sugar in 1 quart of water until dissolved. Cool. Stir-in remaining ingredients and chill.

TEWAHDIDDLE

2 teaspoons brown sugar	1 quart cold beer
½ teaspoon ginger	4 twists lemon peel
2 tablespoons brandy	

DIVIDE sugar, ginger and brandy into 4 glasses and stir until clear. Add beer, while stirring, and float a twist of lemon peel in each glass.

LAMB'S WOOL

4 apples, Macintosh or
  equivalent
1 quart ale
1 pint sweet white wine

Brown sugar to taste
½ teaspoon nutmeg

PUT apples in a pan, cover with foil and bake in 350-degree oven until very soft (about 1 hour). Heat ale and wine, then add sugar and nutmeg. Mash apples through a coarse sieve and mix into the liquid. Stir and reheat. Serve warm to hot.

TO MAKE LEMONADE

6 lemons

3 oranges

1¼ cups sugar
1 tablespoon orange-
  flower water*

PEEL rind very thin from 3 lemons and 1 orange. Pour 2 cups boiling water over rinds and let steep 4 hours. Make juice from the pulp and set aside. Melt sugar in 3 cups boiling water, then combine with juice of all the fruit and the rinds. Stir well. Strain liquid and discard the solids. Stir in orange-flower water and chill until very cold.

* Available from specialty food shops

LEMONADE, ANOTHER WAY

8 lemons　　　　　*2 cups white wine*
1 cup sugar　　　　*Juice of 1 orange*

PEEL the lemons thinly and place peel in a saucepan with 2 cups of water. Squeeze pulp and set juice aside. Bring peels to a boil, remove from heat and strain. Discard peels, stir sugar into liquid, then cool. Add lemon juice, wine, orange juice and water to taste, and chill. Makes approximately 2 quarts.

References

Adam's Luxury and Eve's Cookery, London, 1744. (Facsimile edition by Prospect Books Ltd, London, 1983)

Mrs. Mary Eales's Receipts, 1718. (Facsimile edition by Prospect Books, 1985)

Evelyn, John, **Aceteria**, London, 1699.

Farley, John, **The London Art of Cookery**, 1783

(Glasse, Hannah), **The Art of Cookery Made Plain and Easy**, By a Lady, London, 1747.

Henderson, William, **The Housekeeper's Instructor**, London, c. 1790.

(Kitchiner, William), **The Cook's Oracle**, London, 1822.

MacIver, Susanna, **Cookery and Pastry**, Edinburgh, 1773.

Mason, Charlotte, **The Lady's Assistant**, London 1773.

Moxon, Elizabeth, **English Housewifry**, Leeds, 1764.

Nott, John, **The Cook's and Confectioner's Dictionary**, London, 1723.

Raffald, Elizabeth, **The Experienced English Housekeeper**, Manchester, 1769.

(Rundell, Mrs. Maria Eliza), **A New System of Domestic Cookery**, By a Lady, London, 1807.

Simpson, John, **A Complete System of Cookery**, London, 1806.

Smith, Eliza, **The Compleat Housewife**, London, 1727.

INDEX

INDEX

28 DAYS